making a difference

Caring for the
environment

Jillian Powell

WAYLAND

making a difference

Caring for Others
Caring for the Environment
Caring for Your Pets
Caring for Yourself

Editor: Sarah Doughty
Designer: Jean Wheeler

First published in 1997 by Wayland Publishers Ltd
61 Western Road, Hove, East Sussex BN3 1JD

Find Wayland on the internet at http://www.wayland.co.uk

British Library Cataloguing in Publication Data
Powell, Jillian
Caring for the Environment – (Making a difference)
2. Environmental ethics – Juvenile literature
2. Environmental protection – Citizen participation –
Juvenile literature
I. Title
179.1

ISBN 0 7502 1945 9

Typeset by Jean Wheeler, in England
Printed and bound by G. Canale & C.S.p.A., Turin

Picture acknowledgements
Environmental Images 12, 27, 28 and title page (all by Robert Brook), 16 bottom (V.Miles), 17 (Greg
Abel), 26 bottom (Graham Burns), 29 top and bottom (John Morrison); Impact 6 (Jonathon Pimlott), 7, 9
bottom, 21 top (all by Bruce Stephens), 9 top (Irene Lynch), 16 top (Lional Derimais); Reflections 4, 13
top (both by Jennie Woodcock); RSPCA 19 top (Colin Seddon); Still Pictures 5 bottom, 18, 19 bottom,
21 bottom, 22 (all by Nick Cobbing); Tony Stone Worldwide title page and 24 (Andy Sacks); Wayland
Picture Library 5 top, 8, 9, 10 top, 11, 13 bottom; Zefa 15, 23, 25 top, 25 bottom. Cover commissioned
photography by Angus Blackburn.

Contents

We all share the same world.

The world we live in is called our environment. We must all help to take care of our world.

People like to walk in the city if the streets are kept clean and tidy and free from rubbish.

Parks and gardens are cared for so everyone can enjoy them.

Take care of the environment by not dropping litter in the streets.

Keep the beach
tidy when you
go on holiday.

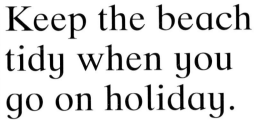

Ugly litter can
spoil the look of
the countryside.

9

Try and save materials like glass, paper, cans and plastics. Reuse them when you can.

Take time to go to the recycling centre with bottles, cans and newspapers.

We all need to save water, especially when there is not much rain.

Think of ways of saving water, like turning the tap off while you are cleaning your teeth.

Take a shower instead of a bath; it uses up less water.

Electricity is supplied
by power stations. Try
and save energy.

You can help by making sure
that things are turned off when
they are not being used.

When shopping,
try to buy things
that don't
have lots of
packaging.

Look out for
packets that are
environmentally
friendly.

You can recycle
packaging by
using it for arts
and crafts.

Food can be farmed in a way that cares for animals and the land.

Organic farmers don't use chemicals to help their fruit or vegetables grow.

Free range means that animals spend some of their time outdoors.

Cars and lorries make
the air we breathe dirty.

Try to walk or cycle
sometimes rather than
going everywhere by car.
It helps keep you fit too!

Noise can spoil the environment. There are lots of different noises in the street.

Help others by keeping quiet sometimes. Enjoy the music you like but remember that others may not want to listen.

We need to take care of trees and plants. You can help look after a garden.

Try planting a tree. Trees help to clean the air we breathe.

Remember trees and hedges are home to insects, birds and animals.

Learning about the environment helps us to know how to take care of it.

You can study plants in a wood or find out about the minibeasts that live in an area.

Study the living things in a stream or river near your home.

It can be fun helping others take care of the environment.

Perhaps you can help create a pond for wildlife to live in.

You can help
clear paths in
the countryside,
or pick up litter.

Whatever you do to help the
environment, you will enjoy it!

Extension activities

MATHS

Conduct surveys to find how pupils travel to school. Which ways cause most pollution? Consider ways of displaying results which encourage people to be environmentally friendly.

What do you eat for packed lunch? How is it packaged? What can be recycled? Illustrate your results in graph form. From your evidence consider ways of reducing waste.

ENGLISH

Caring for the environment is often explored through the media and is the topic for many information books, novels and poetry. Discuss the effectiveness of what you've seen and read. Ask the children to present an important environmental issue in an appropriate medium.

Write letters: to supermarkets asking for changes in over-packaged products or for increased recycling facilities etc.; to Friends of the Earth and Greenpeace to ask for specific information about, for example water pollution; and to the World Wildlife Fund for Nature for information about conservation issues.

Read and look at books such as 'Window' by Jeannie Baker, 'Dinosaurs and All That Rubbish' by Michael Foreman. Discuss how effective they are at conveying environmental issues.

MUSIC

Make a collection of traditional songs, hymns and pop songs that focus on the environment. Which do the children think have most impact and why. Ask them to consider lyrics and tunes. Could they set their own lyrics to music?

HISTORY

Discuss how people in the past treated their environment, such waste disposal, recycling, availability and use of materials, deforestation, water pollution/sewage etc. What comparisons can be made with today? Discuss how aware people were of their actions upon the future environment and what lessons can be learned.

SCIENCE

Using information books research the water cycle. Illustrate it simply and use this to discuss the potential for pollution.

Draw and cut out a variety of food chains and hang them up to illustrate the importance of plant life as the basis for animal life.

Design a winter feeding programme for wild birds. Experiment to see which foods birds prefer. Observe and record the habits of birds visiting the feeding station.

Create a wildlife habitat in your school to encourage insects or pond-life.

ART AND CRAFT

To promote 3D work in school encourage children to recycle all the packaging from home and have a central store of sorted shapes from which children can choose.

Use children's junk modelling as a basis for a wider recycling campaign, which could include the design of posters and other advertising materials.

DESIGN AND TECHNOLOGY

Discuss how children's homes are heated and lit, and methods of conserving energy. Using real and imaginary ideas make annotated drawings of an energy-efficient dwelling.

P.E./DANCE/DRAMA

Choose an environmental issue that could be explored through an improvisation or dance sequence. (Link with music suggestions.)

GEOGRAPHY

Discuss how trade and industry in wealthy counties can affect poorer ones. Write to Oxfam, Tradecraft or Save the Children for information about people affected.

Discuss the irreversible damage caused by some products over which we as consumers have some control, such as destruction of rain forests for hardwood and the undermining of moorland for garden peat.

Establish shared knowledge of weather and seasons in Britain. How does it compare to the weather patterns of other counties? Use this as a basis for discussing the benefits of a moderate climate and constant water supply.

R.E.

Read 'Brother Eagle, Sister Sky' by Susan Jeffries and discuss our moral obligation to care for the environment. Ask children from different religious backgrounds to find examples from holy writing that encourages us to care for our environment.

GEOGRAPHY

- Discussing the effects of world trade.
- Discussing environmental damage.
- Weather patterns.

DESIGN AND TECHNOLOGY

- Designing an energy-efficient home.

ENGLISH

- Discussing media presentation.
- Writing letters.
- Reading environmental stories.
- Presentation.

SCIENCE

- Water pollution.
- Food chains.
- Bird feeding station.

Caring for the Environment
Topic web

HISTORY

- Environment in the past.

MUSIC

- Collecting songs.

R.E.

- Environmental stories.

MATHS

- Conducting a survey.
- Making a graph.

ART AND CRAFT

- 3D work.
- Designing posters.

P.E./DANCE/DRAMA

- Improvisation.

Glossary

energy Power to make things work or move.

litter Rubbish which has been dropped on the ground.

organic A way of farming without using chemicals.

packaging Materials used to wrap up things we buy.

recycling centre A place where you can take glass,
   paper and other materials so that they can be reused.

Books to read

Find Out About: The Environment (BBC Education, 1996)

Going Green at Home and School by John Howson (Wayland, 1993)

My First Green Book by Angela Wilkes (Dorling Kindersley, 1991)

Take One: Why Waste it? (Simon and Schuster, 1991)

These series also have titles about the environment:

Our Green World ... series (Wayland)

The World about Us ... series (Franklin Watts)

What We Can Do About ... series (Franklin Watts)

Index